# THE WIT AND WISDOM OF WALL STREET

by Bill Adler with Bill Adler, Jr.

DOW JONES-IRWIN   Homewood, Illinois 60430

© Bill Adler Books, Inc., 1985

ISBN 0-87094-575-0

Library of Congress Catalog Card No. 83–70857

*Printed in the United States of America*

1 2 3 4 5 6 7 8 9 0 K 2 1 0 9 8 7 6 5

# INTRODUCTION

Its name was taken from an old wall constructed in 1653 by Peter Stuyvesant that stretched across lower Manhattan and was at the time the northernmost boundary of the city. Built to protect Dutch colonists, Wall Street has become synonymous with U.S. capitalism, great wealth, and monetary influence.

Wall Street has evoked great controversy: Admired by many, the Street represents the epitome of the American Dream, the ability of individuals through hard work and imagination to achieve great financial miracles. To others, however, Wall Street symbolizes wealth without compassion, and an ever-growing threat to economic justice.

It is these differing points of view that *The Wit and Wisdom of Wall Street* is about. As important as these issues may be, and as serious as those who argue these positions are, controversy can't avoid producing an occasional humorous thought and provocative idea. While you won't agree with everything contained in these pages, *The Wit and Wisdom of Wall Street* will make you laugh, and, who knows, it may give you the perfect idea you've been looking for.

**Bill Adler**
**Bill Adler, Jr.**

# CONTENTS

# 1

# POLITICIANS LOOK AT WALL STREET

The relationship between American business and government has at times been cordial; on other occasions the two have been great adversaries. Although vast sums of money are frequently at stake, more than merely money has often been involved when these great entities locked horns: principle and raw power were the prizes both sought. From the beginning of this nation's history, politicians have used their influence to control the conduct of business.

— A landed interest, a manufacturing interest, a mercantile interest, a money interest . . . grow up . . . in civilized nations and divide them into different classes actuated by different sentiments and views. The regulation of these various and interfering interests forms the principal task of modern legislation.

James Madison
*The Federalist, No. 10*

1

Politicians Look at Wall Street

— Banking establishments are more dangerous than standing armies.

Thomas Jefferson


— The introduction of a bank . . . has a powerful tendency to extend the active capital of a country . . . It is probable that they will be established wherever they can exist with advantage and wherever they can be supported. If administered with prudence they will add new energies to all pecuniary operations.

Alexander Hamilton
December 5, 1791
New York City


— In the progress of time, and through our own base carelessness and ignorance, we have permitted the money industry, by the virtue of its business, to gradually attain a political and economic influence so powerful that it has actually undermined the authority of the state and usurped the power of democratic government.

Vincent C. Vickers
Director, Bank of England


— What good does it do the world for the governments to sit down at peace tables and to work out the fine political mechanisms if they leave the instruments of economic and technical power in the hands of unrestrained private individuals and corporations?

Harley M. Kilgore
American politician


— I've never been able to understand how the Democrats can run those $1,000-a-plate dinners at such a profit and run the government at such a loss.

Ronald Reagan
Dallas, Texas
October 26, 1967

— A corporation is an artificial being, invisible, intangible, and existing only in the contemplation of the law. Being the mere creature of the law, it possesses only those properties which the charter of its creation confers on it, either expressly or as incidental to its very existence. There are such as are supposed best calculated to effect the object for which it was created. Among the most important are immortality and, if the expression be allowed, individuality; properties by which a perpetual succession of many persons are considered the same and may act as a single individual.

John Marshall
Chief Justice, U.S. Supreme Court
*Dartmouth College* v. *Woodward*
1819

— The true friend of property, the true conservative is he who insists that property shall be the servant and not the master of the commonwealth; who insists that the creature of man's making shall be the servant and not the master of the man who made it. The citizens of the United States must effectively control the mighty commercial forces which they themselves called into being.

Theodore Roosevelt
*The New Nationalism*
1910

— It is to be regretted that the rich and powerful too often bend the acts of government to their selfish purposes.

Andrew Jackson
July 10, 1832

— Corporations have neither bodies to be kicked nor souls to be damned.

Andrew Jackson

— A power has risen up in the government greater than the people themselves, consisting of many and various powerful interests, combined in one mass, and held together by the cohesive power of the vast surplus in banks.

John C. Calhoun
Senate speech
May 27, 1836

— Concentration of wealth and power has been built upon other people's money, other people's business, other people's labor. Under this concentration, independent business was allowed to exist only on sufferance. It has been a menace to . . . American democracy.

Franklin D. Roosevelt
Philadelphia
June 27, 1936

— Prosperity is only an instrument to be used, not a deity to be worshiped.

Calvin Coolidge

— My father always told me that businessmen were sons of bitches.

John F. Kennedy
Washington, D.C.
April 1962

— Every monopoly and all exclusive privileges are granted at the expense of the public, which ought to receive a fair equivalent.

Andrew Jackson
July 10, 1832

— [W]e are gradually reaching a time, if we have not already reached that period, when the business of the country is controlled by men who can be named on the fingers of one hand, because these men control the money of the nation, and that control is growing at a rapid rate. There is only a comparatively small part of it left for them to get, and when they control the money, they control the banks, they control the manufacturing institutions, they control the aviation companies, they control the insurance companies, they control the publishing companies; and we have had some remarkable instances of the control of the publishing companies presented before a subcommittee of the Committee on the Judiciary.

Senator George W. Norris
November 30, 1944


— As we view the achievements of aggregated capital, we discover the existence of trusts, combinations, and monopolies, while the citizen is struggling far in the rear or is trampled to death beneath an iron heel. Corporations, which should be the restrained creatures of the law and the servants of the people, are fast becoming the people's masters.

Grover Cleveland
Annual address to congress
1888


— The notion that a business is clothed with a public interest and has been devoted to the public use is little more than a fiction intended to beautify what is disagreeable to the sufferers.

Oliver Wendell Holmes
*Tyson* v. *Banton*
1927


— You are a den of vipers and thieves. I intend to root you out, and by the eternal God, I will root you out.

Andrew Jackson
1832


— Practices of the unscrupulous money changers stand indicated in the court of public opinion, rejected by the hearts and minds of men . . . The money changers have fled from their high seats in the temple of our civilization. We may now restore the temple to the ancient truths . . . The measure of the restoration lies in the extent to which we apply social values more noble than mere monetary profit . . . The joy and moral stimulation of work no longer must be forgotten in the mad chase of evanescent profits . . . there must be a strict supervision of all the banking and credits and investments; there must be an end to speculation with other people's money.

> Franklin D. Roosevelt
> Inaugural speech
> March 4, 1933

— He smote the rock of the national resources, and abundant streams of revenue gushed forth. He touched the dead corpse of public credit, and it sprang upon its feet.

> Daniel Webster
> On Alexander Hamilton
> 1831

— Many of our rich men have not been content with equal protection and equal benefits but have besought us to make them richer by act of Congress. By attempting to gratify their desires we have in the results of our legislation arrayed section against section, interest against interest, and man against man in a fearful commotion which threatens to shake the foundations of our Union.

> Andrew Jackson
> July 10, 1832

— Whoever controls the volume of money in any country is absolute master of all industry and commerce.

> Abraham Lincoln
> Washington, D.C.
> 1881

Amidst this forest of condemnation, a few kind words for business can be found from certain American politicians:

— We have all heard that if you build a better mousetrap, the world would beat a path to your door. Today, if you build a better mousetrap, the government comes along with a better mouse.

> Ronald Reagan
> Cullman, Alabama
> March 21, 1975

— Government does not solve problems—it subsidizes them.

> Ronald Reagan
> December 11, 1972

— In my country some 25 years ago, you could make a long distance call on a privately owned telephone system from San Francisco to New York for $28. For that same amount of money, you could send 1,376 letters. Today, you can make the same telephone call for two dollars and a half and for that amount you can only send 41 letters. So the government is investigating the Bell system!

> Ronald Reagan
> London, England
> February 2, 1970

— The business of America is business.

> Calvin Coolidge
> January 17, 1925

And borrowing on some well-expressed thoughts, Wendell Wilkie declared:

Politicians Look at Wall Street

— The glory of the United States is business.

Wendell L. Wilkie
September 30, 1940

Still, on issues affecting American business, politicians often strongly disagree. Government borrowing is one issue that still signals great debate.

— A national debt, if it is not excessive, will be to us a national blessing.

Alexander Hamilton
Letter to Robert Morrow
April 30, 1781

— I am one of those who do not believe that a national debt is a national blessing but rather a curse to a republic, inasmuch as it is calculated to raise around the administration a moneyed aristocracy dangerous to the liberties of the country.

Andrew Jackson
April 26, 1824

— If a national debt is considered a national blessing, then we can get on by borrowing. But as I believe it is a national curse, my vow shall be to pay the national debt.

Andrew Jackson
July 10, 1832

— As a very important source of strength and security, cherish public credit, as one method of preserving it is to use it as sparingly as possible, avoiding occasions of expense by cultivating peace.

George Washington
1796

— [C]redit is not only one of the main pillars of the public safety, it is among the principle engines of useful enterprises and internal improvement. As a substitute for capital, it is a little less useful than gold or silver.

Alexander Hamilton
January 16, 1795
New York City

# 2

# WALL STREET LOOKS AT GOVERNMENT AND POLITICS

In the war of words between politicians and business, the men and women of Wall Street usually have the last word.

— The selfish wish to govern is often mistaken for a holy zeal in the cause of humanity.
Elbert Hubbard

— Why is it that businessmen manage their affairs so much more successfully than politicians? Because businessmen have only businessmen to compete with.
Anonymous

— You can't repeal human nature by an act of Congress.
Bernard Baruch

11

Wall Street Looks at Government and Politics

— Government is the only agency that can take a useful commodity like paper, slap some ink in it, and make it totally worthless.

Ludwig Von Mises

— History shows that once the United States government fully recognizes an economic problem and thereby places all its efforts on solving it, the problem is about to be solved by natural forces.

James L. Fraser

— The public be damned.

William H. Vanderbilt

— A creed is an ossified metaphor.

Elbert Hubbard
1927

— Orthodoxy: That peculiar condition where the patient can neither eliminate an old idea nor absorb a new one.

Elbert Hubbard
1927

— You talk about capitalism and communism and all that sort of thing, but the important thing is the struggle everybody is engaged in to get better living conditions, and they are not interested too much in the form of government.

Bernard Baruch
1964

— People may change their minds as often as their coats, and new sets of rules of conduct may be written every week, but the fact remains that human nature has not changed and does not change, that inherent human beliefs stay the same, that fundamental rules of human conduct continue to hold.

Lammot duPont
April 15, 1956

— It is up to businessmen to sell our economic system to the public. They must do as good a job on that as they do on their own products. Unless the advantages of our system over others are brought home to everyone, there is no reason to believe that the trend toward more and more government will be checked.

Joseph Kennedy
December 1945

— We shall have world government whether or not we like it. The only question is whether world government will be achieved by conquest or consent.

James P. Warburg
Washington, D.C.
February 17, 1950

— A political leader must keep looking over his shoulder all the time to see if the boys are still there. If they aren't still there, he's no longer a political leader.

Bernard Baruch
1965

— [P]ower is nothing but a responsibility to do the right thing.

Frank A. Vanderlip

— Politicians have stopped passing the buck—now it stays with them.

Anonymous

Wall Street Looks at Government and Politics

John D. Rockefeller, Grover Whalen, J. P. Morgan, and Cornelius Vanderbilt each expressed significantly different views concerning law and permissible activity.

— I believe that the law was made for man and not man for the law; that government is the servant of the people and not their master.

> John D. Rockefeller, Jr.
> July 21, 1941

— There is plenty of law at the end of a nightstick.

> Grover Whalen
> American businessman

— Anyone has a right to do anything the law does not say is wrong.

> J. Pierpont Morgan

— What do I care about the law. Hain't I got the power?

> Cornelius Vanderbilt

Some businessmen, however, decided to take a more direct approach toward government:

— I needed the goodwill of the legislatures of four states. I "formed" the legislative bodies with my own money. I found that it was cheaper that way.

> Jay Gould
> Testimony before a Congressional Committee

— [Theodore Roosevelt] got down on his knees before us. We bought the SOB, but he didn't stay bought.

> Henry Clay Frick
> 1904

— When I want to buy up any politicians, I always find the antimonopolists the most purchaseable. They don't come so high.

William H. Vanderbilt
October 8, 1882

# 3

# WALL STREET LOOKS AT WORK

Universal among societies, regardless of their political system, is the need to work. Not everyone enjoys working all the time, but Wall Street's successes have come about primarily because of hard work.

— Roasted pigeons don't fly into one's mouth.

> Daniel Guggenheim
> Kennecott Copper

— The real price of everything, what everything really costs to the man who wants to acquire it, is the toil and trouble of acquiring it.

> Adam Smith
> *The Wealth of Nations*
> 1776

17

Wall Street Looks at Work

— Genius is 1 percent inspiration and 99 percent perspiration.

> Thomas Edison
> 1931

— Work is the curse of the drinking class.

> Oscar Wilde

— If a man loves the labor of his trade, apart from any questions of success or fame, the gods have called him.

> Robert Louis Stevenson

— When your work speaks for itself, don't interrupt.

> Henry J. Kaiser

— Each of us has the choice—we must make money work for us, or we must work for money.

> Conrad Leslie

— I'm a great believer in luck, and I find the harder I work, the more I have of it.

> Thomas Jefferson

— When you put your money to work for you, you'd better be prepared to work for it.

> Lewis Owen

Andrew Carnegie liked to talk about his first job:

— The genuine satisfaction I had from that $1.20 outweighs any subsequent pleasure in money-getting.

Andrew Carnegie


Henry Frick offered this advice about achieving success:

— To win in the battle of life a man needs, in addition to whatever ability he possesses, courage, tenacity, and deliberation. He must learn never to lose his head.

Henry Frick


— [W]hat young people should do to avoid temptation: get a job and work at it so hard that temptation would not exist.

Thomas Edison


Although he was talking about hard work, Bernard M. Baruch's thoughts aptly describe a former roommate's cooking techniques:

— Whatever men attempt, they seem driven to overdo.

Bernard Baruch
*Time*
August 19, 1957


— It takes 80 years to make an overnight success.

Eddie Cantor


— You must not suppose, because I am a man of letters, that I never tried to earn an honest living.

George Bernard Shaw

Wall Street Looks at Work

— There will never be a system invented which will do away with the necessity for work.

Henry Ford

— Thinking is the hardest work there is, which is the probable reason why so few engage in it.

Henry Ford

— The effectiveness of work increases according to geometric progression, if there are no interruptions.

Andre Marois

— Work and love—these are the basics. Without them, there is neurosis.

Theodor Reik

— A people so primitive that they did not know how to get money except by working for it.

George Ade

— Work is more fun than fun.

Noel Coward

— He that can work is born a king of something.

Thomas Carlyle

— When white-collar people get jobs, they sell not only their time and energy but their personalities as well. They sell by week or month their smiles and their kindly gestures, and they must practice prompt repression of resentment and aggression.

C. Wright Mills

— Work is not man's punishment; it is his reward and his strength, his glory and his pleasure.

George Saud


— We work to become, not to acquire.

Elbert Hubbard


— The darkest hour of any man's life is when he sits down to plan how to get money without earning it.

Horace Greeley


— Next to doing a good job yourself, the greatest joy is in having someone else do a first-class job under your direction.

William Feather


— Live beyond your means; then you're forced to work hard—you have to succeed.

Edward G. Robinson


— No men living are more worthy to be trusted than those who toil up from poverty, none less inclined to take or touch aught which they have not honestly earned. Let them beware of surrendering a political power which they already possess and which, if surrendered, will surely be used to close the door of advancement against such as they and to fix new disabilities and burdens upon them 'till all of liberty shall be lost.

Abraham Lincoln
Message to Congress
December 3, 1861

# 4

# WALL STREET LOOKS AT BUSINESS

What is a business? Who are these people we call businessmen and businesswomen? Why do some businesses prosper and others fail? Wall Street has had a long time to consider these questions, and while not all the answers are in, some tentative conclusions have been reached.

— The playthings of our elders are called business.
St. Agustine


— A criminal is a person with predatory instincts who has not sufficient capital to form a corporation.
Howard Scott


— Business, more than any other occupation, is a continual dealing with the future: it is a continual calculation, an instinctive exercise in foresight.
Henry R. Luce

Wall Street Looks at Business

Louis Brandeis provided this way of measuring success in business:

— Real success in business is to be found in achievements comparable rather with those of the artist or the scientist, or the inventor or the statesman. And the joys sought in the profession of business must be like their joys and not the mere vulgar satisfaction which is experienced in the acquisition of money, in the exercise of power, or in the frivolous pleasure of mere winning.

> Louis Brandeis
> Brown University
> Providence, Rhode Island
> 1922

— The challenge to things systematically about large, ambiguous questions is inherently daunting and is one that many businessmen—activists by nature—may be reluctant to take up. But if businessmen are to manage events rather than be managed by them, there is no alternative.

> W. S. Rukeyser

— Now that I'm almost up the ladder,
   I should, no doubt, be feeling gladder.
   It is quite fine, the view and such,
   If it just didn't shake so much.

> Richard Armour

— The plain fact is that businessmen do not possess the super qualities which, either in laudation or in condemnation, are frequently attributed to them. They have neither the craftiness and greed with which they are charged nor the profundity and farsightedness with which they are credited.

> Otto H. Kahn
> League for Industrial Democracy,
> New York City
> December 30, 1924

— Entrepreneurial risk-taking is inversely proportional to the size of an organization.

> The Highman de Limut
> Hypotheses

— Don't steal; thoul't never thus compete successfully in business. Cheat.

> Ambrose Bierce
> *The Devil's Dictionary*

— The immense impact of commercial advertising and the mass media of our lives is—let us make no mistake about it—an impact that tends to encourage passivity, to encourage acquiescence and uniformity, to place handicaps on individual contemplativeness and creativeness.

> George F. Kennedy
> Notre Dame University
> May 15, 1953

— Business will be better or worse.

> Calvin Coolidge

— The growth of a large business is merely a survival of the fittest.

> John D. Rockefeller, Sr.

— I've got to keep breathing. It'll be my worst business mistake if I don't.

> Sir Nathan Rothschild
> 1915

— Look, we trade every day out there with hustlers, deal makers, shysters, con men . . . that's the way businesses get started. That's the way this country was built.

> Hubert Allen

Wall Street Looks at Business

— If one defines the term *dropout* to mean a person who has given up serious effort to meet his responsibilities, then every business office, government agency, golf club, and university faculty would yield its quota.

John W. Gardener


— Management is now where the medical profession was when it decided that working in a drug store was not sufficient training to become a doctor.

Lawrence Appley


— Corporations cannot commit treason, nor be outlawed, nor excommunicated, for they have no souls.

Edward Coke


— Whenever you see a successful business, someone once made a courageous decision.

Peter Drucker


— A holding company is the people you give your money to while you're being searched.

Will Rogers


— An executive: A man who can make quick decisions and is sometimes right.

Elbert Hubbard
*A Thousand and One Epigrams*


— To business that we love we rise betime, And go with delight.

William Shakespeare
*Antony and Cleopatra, IV.iv*

— A business conference is a meeting in which everyone says that there is no such thing as a free lunch—while eating one.

A fact

— [T]he Romantic Hero was no longer the knight, the wandering poet, the cowpuncher, the aviator, nor the brave young district attorney but the great sales manager who had an Analysis of Merchandising on his glass-topped desk, whose title of nobility was "go-getter."

Sinclair Lewis
*Babbitt*

— Everything in this country, whether it be commerical or literary, begins with lunch and ends with dinner.

A. Barton Hepburn
Lotus Club, New York City
1911

— The oil business, you know, is liable to sudden and violent fluctuations.

John D. Rockefeller

— Bankruptcy is a legal proceeding in which you put your money in your pants pocket and give your coat to your creditors.

Joey Adams

— Behind every successful man stands a surprised mother-in-law.

Hubert Humphrey

— Well, I don't know as I want a lawyer to tell me what I cannot do. I hire him to tell me how to do what I want to do.

J. P. Morgan

— The question, Who ought to be boss? is like asking, Who ought to be the tenor in the quartet? Obviously, the man who can sing tenor.

Henry Ford

— **Letter to Associates** Gentlemen: You have undertaken to ruin me. I will not sue you, for law takes too long. I will ruin you.

Sincerely,
Cornelius Vanderbilt

— A budget tells us what we can't afford, but it doesn't keep us from buying it.

William Feather

— All business proceeds on beliefs, on judgments of probabilities, and not on certainties.

Charles W. Eliot

— A bank is a place where they lend you an umbrella in fair weather and ask for it back again when it begins to rain.

Robert Frost

— [A] bank's resources should be handled as a general handles his soldiers—you should be strong in reserves. You must be ready to send reinforcements wherever needed. You must send you soldier-dollars wherever they can do the most good.

James Stillman

Profit has always been a primary concern of Wall Street. For some, profit is an evil word, but for most of Wall Street, profits are why they are here.

— Losing potential profits hurts the ego; losing money really hurts.

Gerald Appel

— I believe in profit sharing—I believe it will ultimately settle the labor problem.

Charles M. Schwab

— Civilization and profits go hand in hand.

Calvin Coolidge
November 27, 1920

— Of course I believe in free enterprise, but in my system of free enterprise, the democratic principle is that there never was, never has been, never will be room for the ruthless exploitation of the many for the benefit of the few.

Harry S. Truman
Washington, D.C.
May 9, 1944

Profit, according to Charles M. Schwab, is an important motivating factor for business, but it is not sufficient.

— Business must be profitable if it is to continue to succeed, but the glory of business is to make it so successful that it may do things that are great chiefly because they ought to be done.

Charles M. Schwab

Wall Street Looks at Work

— The society of excess profits for some and small returns for others, the society in which a few prey upon the many, the society in which a few took great advantage and many took great disadvantage must pass.

> Wendell L. Wilkie
> Campaign Speech
> Springfield, Illinois
> October 18, 1940

— The worst crime against working people is a company which fails to operate at a profit.

> Samuel Gompers

— One must now apologize for any success in business as if it were a violation of the moral law so that today it is worse to prosper than to be a criminal.

> Isocrates
> Third century, B.C.

— The trouble with the profit system has always been that it was highly unprofitable to most people.

> E. B. White
> 1944

# 5

# WALL STREET AND TAXES

We are not likely to see a reaction to taxes in America similar in intensity to the Boston Tea Party: on December 16, 1773, colonists demonstrated their opposition to the tax known as the Tea Act of 1773 by dumping chests of tea into Boston harbor during the night. Still, individual citizens, state legislatures, Congress, and a band of hearty professionals known as accountants spend nearly as much money talking about taxes as trying to alter tax schedules. Taxation has been with us through time. In ancient Greece, the Athenians controlled the revenue from publicly owned mines and foreign conquests. Few taxes existed during America's early history. Until 1802 the federal government survived by taxing distilled spirits, sugar, tobacco, slaves, and property sold at auction. It wasn't until Congress needed to fund the War of 1812 that sales tax on gold, silver, jewelry, and watches was introduced. All domestic taxes were abolished from 1817 until 1862 when the high cost of the Civil War forced Congress to enact a system of income taxes and establish the office of Commissioner of Internal Revenue. In 1913, the 16th Amendment to the Constitution granted Congress the power to lay and collect taxes "from whatever source" and on whatever basis it decides. Since then, Congress has legislated tax withholding, corporate taxation, tax cuts, and, of course, the Internal Revenue Service.

Opinions on taxation, while spanning a broad spectrum of philosophies, are almost always strong and reflect points of view that are as deeply rooted as opinions on religion or politics. Yet there is a sense of fatalism involved with talk about taxes. You have to hand it to the tax takers—they're going to get it any way.

Of everything that has been said about taxes, two thoughts remain most famous:

— Taxation without representation is tyranny.

>   James Otis
>   1769

— [I]n this world nothing is certain but death and taxes.

>   Benjamin Franklin
>   Letter to Leroy
>   1789

— Next to being shot at and missed, nothing is quite as satisfying as an income tax refund.

>   F. J. Raymond

Another point of view is bluntly expressed by financier J. P. Morgan:

— Anybody has a right to evade taxes if he can get away with it. No citizen has a moral obligation to assist in maintaining the government. If Congress insists on making stupid mistakes and passing foolish tax laws, millionaires should not be condemned if they take advantage of them.

> J. P. Morgan
> June 15, 1957

— Congress should know how to levy taxes, and if it doesn't know how to collect them, then a man is a fool to pay the taxes.

> J. P. Morgan
> March 6, 1955

Some feelings about taxes are genuinely universal:

— [E]rrors in taxation are visited on everybody.

> Otto Kuhn
> Traffic Club of Pittsburgh,
> Pennsylvania
> April 28, 1921

Alexander Hamilton summed up most people's views of tax like this:

— Taxes are never welcome to a community.

> Alexander Hamilton
> September 19, 1796

— The marvel of all history is the patience which men and women submit to the burdens unnecessarily laid upon them by their governments.

> Senator William E. Borah

— Collecting more taxes than is absolutely necessary is legalized robbery.

> Calvin Coolidge

Wall Street and Taxes

— An unlimited power to tax involves, necessarily, the power to destroy.

> David Webster
> Argument before the Supreme Court
> *McCullough* v. *Maryland*
> 1819

— The power to tax is not the power to destroy while this court sits.

> Oliver Wendell Holmes
> Dissent
> *Panhandle Oil Company* v.
> *Mississippi*
> 1930

— [I]t is essential that you should practically bear in mind that toward the payment of debts there must be revenue; that to have revenue there must be taxes; that no taxes can be devised which are not more or less inconvenient and unpleasant; that the intrinsic embarrassment inseparable from the selection of the proper objects (which is always a choice of difficulties) ought to be a decisive motive for candid construction of the government in making it and for a spirit of acquiescence in the measures for obtaining revenue which the public exigencies may at any time dictate.

> George Washington
> September 19, 1796

— The world's best and safest real estate tax shelter—your own home.

> Chris Welles

— I have some money—not much since I paid my taxes.

> Charles M. Schwab
> Princeton University
> 1920

— He who builds a better mousetrap these days runs into material shortages, patent-infringement suits, work stoppages, collusive bidding, discount discrimination—and taxes.

H. E. Martz

— The income tax has made more liars out of the American people than golf has. Even when you make a tax form out on the level, you don't know, when it's through, if you are a crook or a martyr.

Will Rogers

— The apportionment of taxes on the various descriptions of property is an act which seems to require the most exact impartiality; yet there is, perhaps, no legislative act in which greater opportunity and temptation are given to a predominant party to trample on the rules of justice.

James Madison
*The Federalist, No. 10*

— It's getting harder and harder to support the government in the style to which it has become accustomed.

*Farmer's Almanac*

— Not only is it more blessed to give than receive—it is also deductible.

Anonymous

— The seven deadly sins . . . food, clothing, firing, rent, taxes, respectability, and children.

George Bernard Shaw
Preface, *Major Barbara*
1907

Wall Street and Taxes

— The taxpayer—that's someone who works for the federal government but doesn't have to take a civil service examination.

Ronald Reagan
1968


— The Eiffel Tower is the Empire State Building after taxes.

Anonymous


— The art of taxation consists in so plucking the goose as to get the most feathers with the least hissing.

Jean Baptiste Colbert


— The point to remember is that what the government gives it must first take away.

John S. Coleman


— Governments last as long as the undertaxed can defend themselves against the overtaxed.

Bernard Bereson

# 6

# ECONOMICS AND ECONOMISTS

You can't do much with money without an economy. Of course, some people would argue that you can't accomplish a whole lot these days even with an economy. Nevertheless, economics has a strong, lasting influence on the way we manage our lives.

Who are these latter-day magicians called economists?

— The instability of the economy is equaled only by the instability of economists.

Professor John H. Williams
Harvard University

— If all the economists in the world were laid end to end, they still wouldn't reach a conclusion.

George Bernard Shaw

— Economics is too important to be left to economists.

Louis Stone

Economics and Economists

— The ideas of economists and political philosophers, both when they are right and when they are wrong, are more powerful than is commonly understood. Indeed, the world is ruled by little else.

John Maynard Keynes

Inflation scars the heart muscle of a healthy economy. Although inflation has inspired much debate, no one has found a lasting solution for it.

— There are plenty of good five-cent cigars in the country. The trouble is, they cost a quarter. What the country really needs is a good five-cent nickel.

Franklin Pierce Adams

— These days when you eat out at a fancy restaurant, you need an after-dinner mint—like the one in Denver.

Anonymous

— Inflation is like toothpaste. Once it is out, it's hard to get back in again.

Anonymous

— Deflation to cure inflation is like running over a man with a car and then, to apologize, backing up and running over him again.

Sylvia Porter

During his campaign for governor, Ronald Reagan addressed a group of women in a vegetable-growing region of California:

— You ladies know that if you stand in front of the asparagus counter at the supermarket these days, it's cheaper to eat money.

Ronald Reagan

A clear understanding of unemployment was provided by Calvin Coolidge:

— When more and more people are thrown out of work, unemployment results.

Calvin Coolidge<br>September 29, 1956

— I learned more about economics from one South Dakota dust storm than I did in all my years in college.

Hubert Humphrey

Woody Allen's description of an economics course aptly describes the way many people feel about economics and economists:

— A systematic application and critical evaluation of the basic analytic concepts of economic theory, with an emphasis on money and why it's good. Fixed coefficient production functions, cost and supply curves, and nonconvexity comprise the first semester, with the second semester concentrating on spending, making change, and keeping a neat wallet. The Federal Reserve System is analyzed, and advanced students are coached in the proper method of filling out a deposit slip. Other topics include inflation and depression—how to dress for each, loans, interest, welching.

Woody Allen<br>Copyright © 1967 by Woody Allen.<br>Reprinted from Getting Even,<br>by permission of Random House, Inc.

Economics and Economists

— After order and liberty, economy is one of the highest essentials of a free government . . . Economy is always a guarantee of peace.

Calvin Coolidge
1923

— It is one of the greatest economic errors to put any limitation upon production . . . We have not the power to produce more than there is a potential to consume.

Louis Brandeis
Testimony
U.S. Commission on Industrial
Relations

— A recession is when the other guy loses his job. A depression is when you lose your job. And a panic, that's when your wife losses her job.

Old joke

# 7

# WALL STREET, CAPITALISM, AND THE AMERICAN WAY

Even though our economic system continues to change and flirts with government-socialism on occasion, we are still a country of capitalists. And regardless of one's political beliefs, capitalism has been one of the major forces driving America into the 21st century.

Eric Johnson and Al Capone were not shy about their defense of capitalism:

— [T]he word is *capitalism*. We are too mealymouthed. We fear the word *capitalism* is unpopular. So we talk about the "free enterprise system" and run to cover in the folds of the flag and talk about the American Way of Life.

Eric Allen Johnston<br>Motion picture executive<br>January 26, 1958

— The American system of ours, call it Americanism, call it Capitalism, call it what you like, gives each and every one

Wall Street, Capitalism, and the American Way

of us a great opportunity if we only seize it with both hands
and make the most of it.

Al Capone
1929


Some things do change:

— We declare our opposition to all combinations of
capital, organized as trusts or otherwise.

Republican party
National platform of the
Republican party
1888


— The crippling of individuals I consider the worst evil of
capitalism. Our whole educational system suffers from this
evil. An exaggerated competitive attitude is inculcated into
the student, who is trained to worship acquisitive success as
a preparation for his future career.

Albert Einstein
*Monthly Review*
May 1949


Otto Kahn found this irony in the American system:

— There exists a curious contrast between our attitude
toward the thing called success and toward those corporations or individuals who have contrived conspicuously to
attain it. We inculcate into our youth lessons of industry and
assiduous application, we stimulate their ambitions, we hold
out the incentive of liberal reward to those who, climbing
along the steep road of effort, reach or approach the summit,
we preach the gospel of enterprise, we give popular encour-
agement to the "go-getter" and the "world-beater"—but
when they have accomplished what we have spurred them on
to strive for with all their might, the bricks of criticism,

abuse, and suspicion are apt to fly in profusion around their heads.

Otto Kahn
Authors' League Committee in
Charge of the International
Congress of Motion Picture Arts
June 8, 1923

— The social and economic welfare of the country is inseparably connected with the welfare of its industries.

Otto Kahn
Traffic Club of Pittsburgh
Pittsburgh, Pennsylvania
April 28, 1921

— Democratic capitalism, combined with industrial democracy, is unquestionably the best way of life for mankind.

David J. McDonald
Former president, United
Steelworkers of America
October 30, 1957

— Capitalism has destroyed our belief in any effective power but that of self-interest backed by force.

George Bernard Shaw
*Intelligent Woman's Guide to
Socialism*

— Another thing about capitalism—everybody knows who's in Grant's tomb.

Louis Nelson Bowman

— Big business is basic to the very life of this country; and yet many—perhaps most—Americans have a deep-seated fear and an emotional repugnance to it. Here is monumental contradiction.

David Lilienthal

Wall Street, Capitalism, and the American Way

— Too often the American dream is interrupted by the Japanese alarm clock.

Anonymous

Henry Frick recognized the nature of international business competition.

— Without great, powerful organizations, America cannot hope to compete successfully with the world.

Henry Frick

The marines did more than defend America:

— I spent 33 years [in the Marines] . . . being a high-class muscleman for big business, for Wall Street and the bankers. On shore, I was a racketeer for capitalism . . . I helped purify Nicaragua for the international banking house of Brown Brothers . . . I helped make Mexico . . . safe for American oil interests . . . I brought light to the Dominican Republic for American sugar interests . . . I helped make Haiti and Cuba decent places for National City Bank boys to collect revenue . . . I helped in the rape of half a dozen Central American republics for the benefit of Wall Street. In China . . . I helped see to it that Standard Oil went its way . . . I might have given Al Capone a few hints.

Smedley Butler
U.S. Marine Commander
August 21, 1931

— What is good for General Motors is good for the country, and what is good for the country is good for General Motors.

Charles E. Wilson
Testimony before the Senate Armed
Services Committee
Washington, D.C.
1952

— Private enterprise is ceasing to be free enterprise.

Franklin D. Roosevelt
Washington, D.C.
1938

— The weapon of capital is potentially one of the most powerful and least used in the Western world. Poland affords us a chance to use it. It might turn out to be our only effective way, in the long run, of bringing about change behind the Iron Curtain.

Felix Rohatya
January 11, 1982

— Communism is a hateful thing and a menace to peace and organized government; but the communism of combined wealth and capital, the outgrowth of overweening cupidity and selfishness, which insidiously undermines the justice and integrity of free institutions, is not less dangerous than the communism of oppressed poverty and toil, which, exasperated by injustice and discontent, attacks with wild disorder the citadel of rule.

Grover Cleveland
Annual address to Congress
1888

A Russian high school teacher asked one of his students "How would you characterize the present economic situation of the United States?"

The answer came briskly: "The capitalist American economy is verging on the brink of collapse."

"Excellent, And how would you describe the present economic situation of the Soviet Union?"

This response was offered equally quickly: "The Soviet Union will soon take over the American economy."

Wall Street, Capitalism, and the American Way

— These capitalists generally act harmoniously and in concert to fleece the public.

> Abraham Lincoln
> Springfield, Illinois
> January 1837

— The socialist or anarchist who seeks to overturn present conditions is to be regarded as attacking the foundation upon which civilization itself rests . . . One who studies this subject will soon be brought face-to-face with the conclusion that upon the sacredness of property, civilization itself depends—the right of the laborer to his hundred dollars in the savings bank, and equally the legal right of the millionaire to his millions.

> Andrew Carnegie
> *The Gospel of Wealth*
> 1889

— Remember, my son, that any man who is a bear on the future of this country will go broke.

> J. P. Morgan
> December 10, 1908

# 8

# STOCKS, BONDS, AND INVESTING

Scarcely a month passes without the publication of a new book about investing money. Schemes to invest in real estate on the outskirts of Tibet, speculation on anchovy futures, texts on how to profit from the pending New York City bus and subway fare increase, and discourses on setting up your own $50-million microcomputer business are examples of what authors and their book publishers believe the public is willing to buy. Usually they are right.

But you don't have to look far or spend $4.95 for a paperback copy of *How to Profit from the Next Solar Eclipse* to find wisdom about the stock and bond markets. The few truths about investing are well known to men and women who have made and lost great fortunes in business. Perhaps the best advice is from Benjamin Franklin, who said, "If a man empties his purse into his head, no one can take it from him."

And what about this entity called the stock market? Raymond DeVoe and Blackie Sherrode offer their opinions:

Stocks, Bonds, and Investing

— The stock market is only distantly related to economics. It's a function of greed, apprehension, and panic, all superimposed on the business cycle.

Raymound F. DeVoe, Jr.
Spencer Trask & Company

— If you bet on a horse, that's gambling. If you bet you can make three spades, that's entertainment. If you bet cotton will go up three points, that's business. See the difference?

Blackie Sherrode

Who are these investors anyway? The following few quotations illustrate some common characteristics among investors and among speculators.

— The average prudent investor is a greedy son of a bitch.

Anonymous

— I wish I hadn't acquired respectability. I'd be out selling the market short.

Joe Kennedy
Economic Club of Chicago
1945

— What always impresses me is how much better the relaxed, long-term owners of stocks do with their portfolios than the traders do with their switching of inventory. The relaxed investor is usually better informed and more understanding of essential values; he is more patient and less emotional; he pays smaller annual capital gains taxes; he does not incur unnecessary brokerage commissions; and he avoids behaving like Cassius by "thinking too much."

Lucien D. Hooper
*Forbes* columnist

During the recent market decline, one broker was over-heard asking another, "How are you bearing up under the strain? Do you have trouble sleeping?"

His fellow broker replied, "I sleep like a baby."

The first seemed perplexed. "Like a baby you say?"

He nodded and explained, "I wake up every three hours and cry."

— [T]he responsibility for . . . soaring "ups" and crashing "downs" belongs not to the Stock Exchange as such, because, after all, that institution is essentially a market, and all that those charged with its administration can do is see to it that the goods dealt in are properly labeled, that no face or other-wise objectionable goods are admitted, and that dealings are conducted honestly and with due and watchfully enforced safeguards for the public.

Neither can responsibility be laid justly at the doors of the banks. It is not their function to act as censors and regulators of price movements. [T]he responsibility belongs primarily to those in and out of Wall Street who permit unreflecting desire for gain to make them rush in and buy (being somewhat apt in the process to engage themselves beyond their means) and the same impulse, or unreflecting fear, to rush in and sell. The two very worst counselors in any situation are greed and fear.

Otto Kahn
Atlanta, Georgia
April 23, 1926

Here's the advice:

— In investing, the return you want should depend on whether you want to eat well or sleep well.

J. Kenfield Morley

Stocks, Bonds, and Investing

— If you warn 100 men of possible forthcoming bad news, 80 will immediately dislike you—and if you are so unfortunate to be right, the other 20 will as well.
Anthony Gaubis


— The successful speculator must be content at times to ignore probably two out of every three apparent opportunities to make money.
Charles Dow


— The best investment is land, because they ain't making any more of it.
Will Rogers


— If you don't profit from your investment mistakes, someone else will.
Yale Hirsch


— Gentlemen prefer bonds.
Andrew Mellon


— Invest in inflation. It's the only thing going up.
Will Rogers


— A broker is a man who runs your fortune into a shoestring.
Alexander Woolcott


— If a man saves $15 a week and invests in good common stocks and allows the dividends and rights to accumulate, at the end of 20 years he will have at least $80,000. He will have an income from investments of around $400 a month. He will be rich. And because income can do that, I am firm in my belief that anyone not only can be rich but ought to be rich.

John J. Raskob
1928

— Never follow the crowd.

Bernard Baruch
February 25, 1957

— When you lose on the stock market, don't blame the bulls and bears but the bum steers.

Anonymous

— A study of economics usually reveals that the best time to buy anything is last year.

Marty Allen

No matter what the theme of his speeches or the basis of his financial policies, Joe Kennedy, chairman of the Security and Exchange Commission, always kept a clear-eyed view of his colleagues on Wall Street. There were those who claimed gamblers and speculators were one in the same sort. Joe Kennedy saw them as two distinct types:

— I think the primary motive in back of most gambling is the excitement of it. While gamblers naturally want to win, the majority of them derive pleasure even if they lose. The desire to win, rather than the excitement involved, seems to me to be the compelling force behind speculation.

Joe Kennedy
January 18, 1936

Stocks, Bonds, and Investing

— There are old traders around and bold traders around, but there are no old, bold traders around.

Bob Dinda
Merrill Lynch


— A man cannot be a good doctor and keep telephoning his broker between patients nor a good lawyer with his eye on the ticker.

Walter Lippman


— If you hear that "everybody" is buying a certain stock, ask who is selling.

James Dines


— To speculate in Wall Street when you are not an insider is like buying cows by candlelight.

Daniel Drew


— It is wise to remember that too much success [in the stock market] is in itself an excellent warning.

Gerald M. Loeb


— When a company president is ready to buy you lunch, it's time to sell the stock. When he has something really good, you can't get him on the phone.

Phil Stoller


— The stock market has spoiled more appetites than bad cooking.

Will Rogers

— Committees seem to be as poor in selecting stocks as in composing sonnets.

Murphy Teigh Bloom

— Don't confuse brains with a bull market.

Humphrey Neill

— Select stocks the way porcupines make love—very carefully.

Robert Dinda<br>Merrill Lynch

— If you are considering the purchase of a particular stock but aren't happy with its current price, just wait a minute.

Anonymous

— You have to watch out for the railroad analyst who can tell you the number of ties between New York and Chicago but not when to sell Penn Central.

Nicholas Thorndike

— October—This is one of the peculiarly dangerous months to speculate in stocks. Others are November, December, January, February, March, April, May, June, July, August, and September.

Mark Twain

— Never invest your money in anything that eats or needs repairing.

Billy Rose

# 9

# WALL STREET TALKS ABOUT BEING RICH

What is it like to be rich? The super-rich have definite points of view on how it feels to be wealthy. And so, naturally, do the not-so-rich, whose opinions on this subject are also pointed.

— The rich get richer and the poor get poorer.
Andrew Carnegie

— Great wealth always supports the party in power no matter how corrupt it may be. It never exerts itself for reform, for it instinctively fears change.
Henry George<br>Social Progress

— [U]pon the sacredness of property, civilization itself depends—the right of the laborer to his hundred dollars in the savings bank, and equally the legal right of the millionaire to his millions. This, then, is held to be the duty of the men of wealth: First, to set an example of modest un- ostentatious living, shunning display or extravagance; to provide moderately for the legitimate wants of those de- pendent upon him; and after doing so consider all surplus revenues which come to him simply as trust funds, which he is called upon to administer, and strictly bound as a matter of duty to administer in the manner which, in his judgment, is best calculated to produce the most beneficial results for the community—the man of wealth thus becoming the mere agent and trustee for his poorer brethren, bringing to their service his superior wisdom, experience, and ability to ad- minister, doing for them better than they would or could do for themselves. [T]he millionaire will be but a trustee of the poor, entrusted for a season with a great part of the increased wealth of the community but administering it for the com- munity far better than it could or would have done for itself.

Andrew Carnegie
*The Gospel of Wealth*
1889


— You are affluent when you buy what you want, do what you wish, and don't give a thought to what it costs.

J. P. Morgan


— I'm opposed to millionaires, but it would be dangerous to offer me the position.

Mark Twain


— [The wealthy] are indeed rather possessed by their money than possessors.

Robert Burton
*Anatomy of Melancholy*

— If you want to know what God thinks of money, just look at the people she gives it to.

Anonymous

— People of privilege will always risk their complete destruction rather than surrender any material part of their advantage.

John Kenneth Galbraith

— A man is rich in proportion to the things he can afford to let alone.

Henry David Thoreau

— I'm so happy to be rich, I'm willing to take all the consequences.

Howard Abramson

— It isn't enough for you to love money—it's also necessary that money should love you.

Baron Rothschild

— The petty economics of the rich are just as amazing as the silly extravagances of the poor.

William Feather

— Make money, and the whole world will conspire to call you a gentleman.

Mark Twain

Wall Street Talks about Being Rich

— If a free society cannot help the many who are poor, it cannot save the few who are rich.

John F. Kennedy

— Few of us can stand prosperity. Another man's, I mean.

Mark Twain

— Riches enlarge rather than satisfy appetites.

Thomas Fuller

— I have enough money to get by. I'm not independently wealthy, just independently lazy, I suppose.

Montgomery Cliff

— I have no complex about wealth. I have worked hard for my money, producing things people need. I believe that the able industrial leader who creates wealth and employment is more worthy of historical notice than politicians or soldiers.

Paul Getty

— I was born into it, and there was nothing I could do about it. It was there, like air or food or any other element. The only question with wealth is what you do with it.

John D. Rockefeller

— I wish to become rich so that I can instruct the people and glorify honest poverty a little, like those kindhearted, fat, benovelent people do.

Mark Twain

— Money is honey, my little sonny,
    And a rich man's joke is always funny.
                                    T. E. Brown

— The man who dies rich dies disgraced.
                                    Andrew Carnegie
                                    *The Gospel of Wealth*
                                    1889

— The richer and bigger you are, the more considerate you have to be of other people's feelings if you are to succeed in taking the curse off being rich.
                                    J. Ogdon Symour
                                    Armour & Co.

— The problem of our age is the proper administration of wealth so that the ties of brotherhood may still bind together the rich and the poor in harmonious relationships.
                                    Andrew Carnegie
                                    *The Gospel of Wealth*
                                    1889

How rich is rich?

— If you can actually count your money, then you are not really a rich man.
                                    Paul Getty

— It doesn't matter if you're rich or poor—as long as you've got money.
                                    Joe E. Lewis

Wall Street Talks about Being Rich

— People's spending habits depend more on how wealthy they feel than with the actual amount of their current income.

A. C. Pigou

— A man who has money may be anxious, depressed, frustrated and unhappy, but one thing he's not—and that's broke.

Brendan Francis

— Some folks seem to get the idea that they're worth a lot of money just because they have it.

Seth Parker

— With the great part of rich people, the chief employment of riches consists in the parade of riches, which, in their eye, is never so complete as when they appear to possess those decisive marks of opulence which nobody can possess but themselves.

Adam Smith
*The Wealth of Nations*
1776

— He frivols through the livelong day,
  He knows not Poverty, her pinch.
  His lot seems light, his heart seems gay;
  He has a cinch.

Franklin P. Adams
*The Rich Man*

— The meek shall inherit the earth, but not its mineral rights.

J. Paul Getty

# 10

# THE POOR

— The government says two can live on $8,000 a year, but they don't say two what.

Anonymous

— No one can worship God or love his neighbor on an empty stomach.

Woodrow Wilson
New York City
May 23, 1912

— I've been rich, and I've been poor; rich is better.

Sophie Tucker

The Poor

— I'd like to live like a poor man with lots of money.

Pablo Picasso


— [U]mble we are, 'umble we have been, 'umble we shall ever be.

Charles Dickens
*David Copperfield*


— He has so much money that he could afford to look poor.

Edgar Wallace


— He was subject to a kind of disease which, at that time, they called lack of money.

Francois Rabelais


— One of the strangest things about life is that the poor, who need money the most, are the very ones that never have it.

Finley Peter Dunne


— No men living are more worthy to be trusted than those who toil up from poverty, none less inclined to take or touch aught which they have not honestly earned. Let them beware of surrendering a political power which they already possess and which, if surrendered, will surely be used to close the door of advancement against such as they and to fix new disabilities and burdens upon them till all of liberty shall be lost.

Abraham Lincoln
Message to Congress
December 3, 1861

— The engine and transmission and the wheels
Are made of greed, fear, and invidiousness,
Fueled by superpep high-octane money
And lubricated with hypocrisy.
Interior upholstery is all handsewn
Of the skins of children of the very poor.
Justice and mercy, charity and peace
Are optional items at slight extra cost.
The steering gear is newsprint powered by
Expediency but not connected with
The wheels, and finally, there are no brakes.
However, the rearview mirror and the horn
Are covered by our lifetime guarantee.

Howard Nemerov
*"The Great Society, Mark X"*
from *The Collected Poems of
Howard Nemerov.* University of
Chicago Press, 1977. Reprinted
by permission of the author.

— There is nothing more demoralizing than a small but adequate income.

Edward Wilson

— The crying need of the nation is not for better morals, cheaper bread, temperance, liberty, culture, redemption of fallen sisters and erring brothers, not the grace, love, and fellowship of the trinity, but simply for enough money. And the evil to be attacked is not sin, suffering, greed, priestcraft, kingcraft, demagogy, monopoly, ignorance, drink, war, pestilence, nor any of the consequences of poverty, but just poverty itself.

George Bernard Shaw
Preface, *Major Barbara*
1907

— I haven't heard of anybody who wants to stop living on account of the cost.

Kim Hubbard

The Poor

— The man who dies leaving behind him millions of available wealth, which was his to administer during his life, will pass away "unwept, unhonored, and unsung" no matter to what uses he leaves the dross which he cannot take with him. Of such as these the public verdict will then be: "The man who dies thus rich dies disgraced."

Such, in my opinion, is the true Gospel concerning Wealth, obedience to which is destined some day to solve the problem of the Rich and the Poor, and to bring "Peace on earth, among men Good Will."

Andrew Carnegie
*The Gospel of Wealth*
1889


— No society can surely be flourishing and happy of which the far greater part of the members are poor and miserable.

Adam Smith
*The Wealth of Nations*
1776

# 11

# WALL STREET
# AND LABOR

The relationship between management and labor has, on occasion, been friendly. At times, the struggle between bigger profits and workers' rights has been bitter. Each side considers itself to be fully justified in pursuing its goals: The spirit of cooperation and compromise has been hard to attain.

Nevertheless, labor and management have made great progress over the past two centuries in working toward mutually beneficial interests. Wall Street's views of labor tell much about America's history.

One of the fundamental questions affecting the worker-management relationship is "Who is responsible for production?"

— Every manufacturer ought to remember that his fortune was not achieved by himself alone but by the cooperation of his workmen. He should acknowledge their rights to share the benefits of that which could not exist without their

Wall Street and Labor

faithful performance of duty. Not until the capitalist is just
enough to recognize this truth can he ever join a group of
workmen and feel himself among his friends.

Peter Cooper

— The production of wealth is not the work of any one
man, and the acquisition of great fortunes is not possible
without the cooperation of multitudes of men.

Peter Cooper
1892

— Men, not machinery or plants, make an organization.

John D. Rockefeller

— It is not the employer who pays the wages—he only
handles the money. It is the product that pays wages.

Henry Ford

Henry Ford's opinion of labor, however, was not very
progressive.

— Labor unions are the worst thing that ever struck the
earth, because they take away a man's independence.

Henry Ford
Ford Motor Co. publication
1936

— Show me the country in which there are no strikes, and
I'll show you that country in which there is no liberty.

Samuel Gompers
Labor leader

— I should like to see our country unionized to the hilt.

Frank Lloyd Wright
May 2, 1959

— It is essential that there should be organizations of labor. This is an era of organization. Capital organizes, and therefore labor must organize.

Theodore Roosevelt
Milwaukee, Wisconsin
October 14, 1912


Charles Schwab recognized the need to get management and labor to work together.

— [I]f the managers of industry can develop some universal plan which will make labor not only well paid but happy in doing the work itself, one of the greatest possible boons to mankind will have been realized.

Charles M. Schwab


— Labor: One of the processes by which A acquires property of B.

Ambrose Bierce
*The Devil's Dictionary*


— You can't mine coal without machine guns.

Richard Mellon
Congressional testimony
June 14, 1937


— I believe in the dignity of labor, whether with head or hand; that the world owes no man a living, but that it owes every man an opportunity to make a living.

John D. Rockefeller
July 21, 1941


— And we heard a report about one employer who had all his employees X-rayed to see how much work they had left in them.

Anonymous

Wall Street and Labor

The president of Chile was having some difficulty controlling worker unrest, so he paid a visit to France to buy some tanks. Moments after he had concluded his meeting with the tank company director, the lunch-time siren sounded. Fear visited the president's eyes as he watched hundreds of workers drop their tools, leave the machinery unattended, and rush out of the factory. "Let's escape!" The president pleaded. "The workers are rioting. If we can reach one of your tanks, we can fight our way to safety."

"You don't have to worry," the managing director replied calmly. "It happens every day. In 45 minutes, another siren will sound, and they will all rush back to work."

"Fantastic," Chile's president said. "Forget the tanks. I'll take 5,000 sirens instead."

— It is all one to me if a man comes from Sing Sing or Harvard. We hire a man, not his history.

Henry Ford

— S'pose you got a job a work an' there's jus' one fella wants the job. You got to pay 'im what he asts. But s'pose they's a hundred men wants that job. S'pose them men got kids an' them kids is hungry. S'pose a nickle 'll byt leas' sompin for the kids. An' you got a hundred men. Jus' offer 'em a nickel—why, they'll kill each other fightin' for that nickel.

John Steinbeck
*The Grapes of Wrath*

— The employer puts his money into . . . business and the workman his life. The one has as much right as the other to regulate that business.

Clarence S. Darrow
*The Railroad Trainman*
November 1909

— When white-collar people get jobs, they sell not only their time and energy but their personalities as well. They sell by week or month their smiles and their kindly gestures, and they must practice prompt repression of resentment and aggression.

C. Wright Mills

— **Question:** Do you consider $10 a week enough for a longshoreman with a family to support?

**Morgan:** If that's all he can get, and he takes it, I should say it's enough.

J. P. Morgan
Testimony, U.S. Commission on
Industrial Relations

# 12

# WALL STREET LOOKS AT PROGRESS

Wall Street, its critics, and its admirers share a common interest in progress. Not everyone looks at progress in the same light, but most people on and off Wall Street are equally fascinated by how this process occurs.

— We make progress at night while the politicians sleep.
Brazilian peasant proverb

— I don't know where speculation got a bad name, since I know of no forward leap which was not fathered by speculation.
John Steinbeck

— Even responsible dissent may not be a welcome element on every occasion, but the first point I want to make is that it is absolutely essential to progress. Without the change bred by honest and enlightened dissent, man is bound to die in mind, spirit, and body. It is his unique ability to be dissatisfied that imbues him with dedication and drive required for the enlightenment of all great works.

David Rockefeller
Commencement speech
Choate School
1967

— Great pioneers like Huntington and Hill, men of daring and constructive genius like Harriman . . . did mighty work. True, they reaped rich rewards, but the wealth they received was but a trifling fraction of the wealth their work created for the people.

Otto H. Kahn
Traffic Club of Pittsburgh,
Pennsylvania
April 28, 1921

— Technological progress has merely provided us with more efficient means for going backwards.

Aldous Huxley

— A man with a new idea is a crank—until the idea succeeds.

Mark Twain

— And while the law [of competition] may be sometimes hard for the individual, it is best for the race, because it ensures the survival of the fittest in every department. We accept and welcome, therefore, as conditions to which we must accommodate ourselves, great inequality of environment, the concentration of business, industrial and commercial, in the hands of a few, and the law of competition between these, as being not only beneficial but essential for the future progress of the race.

Andrew Carnegie
*The Gospel of Wealth*
1889

— We might as well urge the destruction of the highest existing type of man, because he failed to reach our ideal as to favor the destruction of Individualism, Private Property, the Law of Accumulation of Wealth, and the Law of Competition; for these are the highest results of human experience, the soil in which society has so far produced the best fruit.

Andrew Carnegie
*The Gospel of Wealth*
1889

— Not blind opposition to progress, but opposition to blind progress.

Sierra Club

— The world hates change, yet it is the only thing that has brought progress.

Charles F. Kettering

— Orthodoxy: That peculiar condition where the patient can neither eliminate an old idea nor absorb a new one.

Wilbert Hubbard
1927

— The American beauty rose can be produced in all its splendor only by sacrificing the early buds that grow up around it.

John D. Rockefeller

Wall Street Looks at Progress

— The reason men oppose progress is not because they hate progress, but they love inertia.

Elbert Hubbard
1927

— Those who have never made a mistake work for those who have dared to.

Leon Sokolsky

— Everybody says what business needs is confidence . . . confidence that if business does the right thing it will be protected and given a chance to live, make profits, and grow, helping itself and helping the country.

Joe Kennedy
National Press Club
July 25, 1943

— We who are bankers are afforded an opportunity to sit beside the highway of business and watch the caravan of industry pass. We see it reach to the end of the known road and strike boldly across the broad and unmarked plains of the unknown future. Sometimes we are in a position to accelerate the speed of progress of some particular aggressive driver in the ranks of this big parade.

Paul Mazur
New York City
January 1928

# 13

# WALL STREET LOOKS AT CHARITY

Accumulated wealth has helped inspire philanthropy. While charity can never end the economic ills that permeate our society, it has helped millions of people.

— Philanthropist: A rich (and usually bald), old gentleman who has trained himself to grin while his conscience is picking his pocket.

Ambrose Bierce

— The best philanthropy is a search for cause, an attempt to cure evils at their source.

John D. Rockefeller

When William Allen White, the founder of Emporia Gazette, gave 50 acres of park land to his home town, he said,

— This is the last kick in a fistful of dollars I am getting rid of. I have tried to teach people that there are three kicks in every dollar: one, when you make it—and how I love to make a dollar; two, when you have it—and I have the Yankee lust for saving. The third kick is when you give it away—and it is the biggest kick of all.

William Allen White


— The good Lord gave me my money, and how could I withhold it from the University of Chicago?

John D. Rockefeller, Sr.
Address to the graduating class


— This, then, is held to be the duty of the man of wealth: First, to set an example of modest, unostentatious living, shunning display or extravagance; to provide moderately for the legitimate wants of those dependent upon him; and after doing so consider all surplus revenues which come to him simply as trust funds, which he is called upon to administer, and strictly bound as a matter of duty to administer in the manner which, to his judgment, is best calculated to produce the most beneficial results for the community—the man of wealth thus becoming the mere agent and trustee for his poorer brethren, bringing to their service his superior wisdom, experience, and ability to administer, doing for them better than they would or could for themselves.

Andrew Carnegie
*The Gospel of Wealth*
1889


— Being very rich, as far as I am concerned, is having a margin. The margin is being able to give.

May Sarton
*Journal of a Solitude*

— I believe the power to make money is a gift of God . . . to be developed and used to the best of our ability for the good of mankind. Having been endowed with the gift I possess, I believe it is my duty to make money and still more money and to use the money I make for the good of my fellow man according to the dictates of my conscience.

John D. Rockefeller

— You can be social minded without being a socialist.

Charles E. Wilson
Address
Dartmouth College
May 5, 1959

— Those who would administer wisely, must, indeed, be wise, for one of the serious obstacles to the improvement of our race is indiscriminate charity.

Andrew Carnegie
*The Gospel of Wealth*
1889

— Not only is it more blessed to give than receive—it is also deductible.

Anonymous

— The man who dies leaving behind him millions of available wealth, which was his to administer during life, will pass away "unwept, unhonored, and unsung," no matter to what uses he leaves the dross which he cannot take with him. Of such as these the public verdict will then be: "The man who dies thus rich dies disgraced." Such, in my opinion, is the true Gospel concerning Wealth, obedience to which is destined some day to solve the problem of the Rich and the Poor, and to bring "Peace on earth, among men Good Will."

Andrew Carnegie
*The Gospel of Wealth*
1889

— We must all do what we can to save food for the millions who are suffering starvation.

John D. Rockefeller

— Capital punishment is as fundamentally wrong as a cure for crime as charity is wrong as a cure for poverty.

Henry Ford

# 14

# MONEY

Money is a symbol and a tool; it is also a system of measurement. But what does money measure? Money can be translated into numerous and varied units. For example, $100 can buy a certain number of chickens, several magazine subscriptions, a pleasant evening out, or it can be invested carefully. Even money's value is hard to determine. To a millionaire, $10 is a trifle; to the poor, this same sum can buy precious heat for the winter or can put another meal on the table. Money has caused great happiness; but it is strange that this same substance has also produced misery. It is often difficult to get and sometimes hard to get rid of.

Much effort has been dedicated toward trying to define and explain money.

— Money is the most important thing in the world. It represents health, strength, honor, generosity, and beauty as conspicuously as the want of it represents illness, weakness, disgrace, meanness, and ugliness.

George Bernard Shaw
Preface, *Major Barbara*
1907

— Money, it turned out, was exactly like sex; you thought of nothing else if you didn't have it and thought of other things if you did.

James Baldwin

— Money is the poor people's credit card.

Marshall McLuhan

— Money is always there, but the pockets change; it is not in the same pockets after a change, and that is all there is to say about money.

Gertrude Stein

Senator Robert Owen of Oklahoma explained the frustrations he and his colleagues faced whenever they tried to revise the currency and banking laws. The hardest part was selecting a commodity of universal value with which to back the currency:

— [M]en . . . insisted that the true standard of value was the kilowatt-hour.

Senator Robert Owen
Economic Club, New York City
November 10, 1913

Henry Ford looked at money this way:

— Money doesn't do me any good. I can't spend it on myself. Money has no value, anyway. It is merely a transmitter, like electricity.

Henry Ford

— When a man says money can do anything, that settles it: he hasn't any.

W. E. Howe

— To make money, make quantity.

Henry Ford

In business, according to Otto Kahn, some elements are more powerful than money.

— [T]he most serviceable of all assets is reputation . . . it works for you automatically . . . 24 hours a day. Unlike money, reputation cannot be bequeathed. It is always personal. It must be acquired. Brains alone, however brilliant, cannot win it.

Otto Kahn
Harvard Club
New York City
November 13, 1924

— There is no fortress so strong that money cannot take it.

Cicero

— When one has had to work so hard to get money, why should he impose on himself the further hardship of trying to save it?

Don Herold

Money

— When I was young, I used to think that money was the most important thing in life; now that I am old, I know it is.

Oscar Wilde

If you don't have money, you can always borrow someone else's.

— It saves a lot of trouble if instead of having to earn money and save it, you can just go and borrow it.

Winston Churchill

— If you would know the value of money, go to try to borrow some.

Benjamin Franklin

— Neither a borrower or a lender be:
For loan oft loses both itself and friend,
And borrowing dulls the edge of husbandry.

Shakespeare
*Hamlet I, iii*

— Money talks, and it is the only conversation worth hearing when times are bad.

Fred Allen

Money is not virtuous in everyone's opinion.

— Gold in families debate;
Gold does friendship separate;
Gold does civil war create.

Abraham Cowley
*Anacreonitics: Gold*

— Money, which represents the prose of life and which is hardly spoken of in parlors without an apology, is, in its effects and laws, as beautiful as roses.

Ralph Waldo Emerson


— A creditor is worse than a master, for a master owns only your person—a creditor owns your dignity and can belabor that.

Victor Hugo
*Les Miserables*


— When it is a question of money, everybody is of the same religion.

Voltaire


— Let all the learned say what they can, 'Tis ready money that makes the man.

William Somerville
*Ready Money*


— Up and down the City Road, in and out the Eagle, That's the Way the money goes—pop goes the weasel!

W. R. Mandale
*Pop Goes the Weasel*


— Put not your trust in money, but put your money in trust.

Oliver Wendell Holmes


— Money is like an arm or a leg—use it or lose it.

Henry Ford
November 8, 1931

Money

— Never ask of money spent
  Where the spender thinks it went.
  Nobody was ever meant
  To remember or invent
  What he did with every cent.

> Robert Frost
> *The Hardship of Accounting*


— People's spending habits depend more on how wealthy they feel than with the actual amount of their current income.

> A. C. Pigou


— That most delicious of all privileges—spending other people's money.

> John Randolph


— When you see a situation you cannot understand, look for the financial interest.

> Representative Tom L. Johnson


— Money is so unlike every other article that I believe a man has neither a legal or a moral right to take all that he can get.

> Peter Cooper
> 1892


— What's money? It's the only thing that's handier than a credit card.

> Anonymous

— O money, money, money,
I'm not necessarily one of those who
think thee holy.
But I often stop to wonder how thou canst go out so
fast when
thou comest so slowly.

Ogden Nash


— Golden shackles are far worse than iron ones.

Mohandus Ghandhi


— Gold is the most useless thing in the world. I am not interested in money but in the things of which money is merely a symbol.

Henry Ford


— Anyone who tries to understand the money question goes crazy.

Frank Vanderlip


— All thinges obeyen to moneye.

Geoffrey Chaucer
*The Tale of Melibus*


— Money is like the reputation for ability—more easily made than kept.

Samuel Butler


— Why doesn't someone write a poem on money? Nobody does anything but abuse it. There's hardly a good word for money to be found in literature. The poets and writers have been needy devils and thought to brave out their beggary by pretending to despise it. This shows what liars poets and literary men are.

The chief cry of their hearts has never found its way into their books during the last 3,000 years.

John Jay Chapman

— The only people who claim that money is not important are people who have enough money so that they are relieved of the ugly burden of thinking about it.

Joyce Carol Oates

— The chief value of money lies in the fact that one lives in a world in which it is overestimated.

H. L. Mencken

# 15

# WALL STREET LOOKS AT LIFE

There are distinctly human and philosophical sides to the men and women of business. Their views on family, friends, happiness, and religion provide insight into the way business in America is run.

— The measure of a man's success in life is not the money he's made—it's the kind of family he has raised.

Joe Kennedy
September 7, 1957

— Old age is always 15 years older than I am.

Bernard Baruch

— Inherited wealth is a big handicap to happiness. It is as certain death to ambition as cocaine is to morality.

William K. Vanderbilt
1905

Wall Street Looks at Life

— Real difficulties can be overcome; it is only the imaginary ones that are unconquerable.

> Theodore N. Vail
> American Telephone and Telegraph

— I believe in the supreme worth of the individual and in his right to life, liberty, and the pursuit of happiness.

> John D. Rockefeller
> July 21, 1941

— Money doesn't make you happy, but it quiets the nerves.

> Sean O'Casey

— Everyone likes to think that he has done reasonably well in life so that it comes as a shock to find our children believing differently. The temptation is to tune them out; it takes much more courage to listen.

> John D. Rockefeller III

Andrew Carnegie's partner, Henry Clay Frick, believed that overspoiling children was wrong:

— I do not believe in leaving children a great many millions of dollars.

> Henry Frick

— The gods are those who either have money or do not want it.

> L. Butler

— I do not believe that any type of religion should ever be introduced into the public schools of the United States.

Thomas Edison
Commencement address
University of Chicago
1895

— Where Vanderbilt sits, there is the head of the table. I teach my son to be rich.

William H. Vanderbilt

— Don't forget until too late that the business of life is not business but living.

B. C. Forbes

— It's a kind of spiritual snobbery that makes people think they can be happy without money.

Albert Camus

— There are only two pursuits that get into your blood—politics and the motion picture business.

Joe Kennedy
*Time*
August 12, 1940

— The happiest time in any man's life is when he is in red-hot pursuit of a dollar with a reasonable prospect of overtaking it.

Josh Billings

— Annual income twenty pounds, annual expenditure nineteen nineteen six, result happiness. Annual income twenty pounds, annual expenditure twenty pounds ought and six, result misery.

Charles Dickens
*David Copperfield*

And what about after life? One common theme emerges:

— If your riches are yours, why don't you take them with you to t' other world?

Benjamin Franklin
*Poor Richard's Almanac*
1751

— You can't take it with you.

Moss Hart and George Kaufman
1936

— True, you can't take it with you, but then that's not the place where it comes in so handy.

Brendan Francis

# 16

# THE FUTURE

All business is directed toward the future and what the future will be like—how the economy will fare, what new markets can develop, changes in inflation, and the condition of the environment play an important role in business decisions.

— My interest is in the future, because I'm going to spend the rest of my life there.

C. F. Kettering

— We pay the debts of the last generation by issuing bonds payable by the next generation.

Lawrence J. Peter

— [I]n all likelihood we must brace ourselves for the consequences of . . . "wars of redistribution" or of "preemptive

The Future

seizure," the rise of social tensions in the industrialized nations over the division of an ever more slow-growing or even diminishing product, and the prospect of a far more coercive exercise of national power as the means by which we will attempt to bring these disruptive processes under control . . . Rationalize as we will, stretch the figures as favorably as honestly will permit, we cannot reconcile the requirements for a lengthy continuation of the present rate of industrialization of the globe with the capacity of existing resources of the fragile biosphere to permit to tolerate the effects of that industrialization . . . If, then, by the question, Is there hope for man? we ask whether it is possible to meet the challenges of the future without the payment of a fearful price, the answer must be: No, there is no such hope.

Robert Heilbroner
Economist *An Inquiry Into the Human Prospect*
1975, © W. W. Norton & Co.


— I know of no way of judging the future by the past.

Patrick Henry


— The reasonable man adapts himself to the world; the unreasonable one persists in trying to adapt the world to himself. Therefore, all progress depends on the unreasonable man.

George Bernard Shaw


— Yesterday is a canceled check, tomorrow is a promissory note, today is ready cash.

Hubert Tinley


— What has destroyed every previous civilization has been the tendency to the unequal distribution of wealth and power. This same tendency, operating with increasing force, is observable in our civilization today, showing itself in every progressive community, and with greater intensity the more progressive the community.

Henry George
*Progress and Poverty*
1879


— There's the story about the Wall Street whiz kid who lost his money and half his friends. The other half didn't know he lost his money.

Anonymous